The Ulti Salad Recipe Book

Quick and Easy to Prepare Salad Recipes You'd Love

BY: SOPHIA FREEMAN

© 2019 Sophia Freeman All Rights Reserved

COPYRIGHTED

Liability

This publication is meant as an informational tool. The individual purchaser accepts all liability if damages occur because of following the directions or guidelines set out in this publication. The Author bears no responsibility for reparations caused by the misuse or misinterpretation of the content.

Copyright

The content of this publication is solely for entertainment purposes and is meant to be purchased by one individual. Permission is not given to any individual who copies, sells or distributes parts or the whole of this publication unless it is explicitly given by the Author in writing.

Table of Contents

Introduction 7

Caesar Pasta Salad 10

Chicken Kale Salad.. 14

Apple Spinach Salad with Chicken Strips 17

Asian Chicken Salad.. 20

Chicken Salad with Brussels Sprouts Mushroom............... 23

Caesar Salad with Tofu 26

Beet Salad 29

Fresh Green Salad... 32

Greek Salad.. 35

Cranberry Salad.. 38

Orange Raspberry Salad 41

Avocado Salad with Lime Cilantro Dressing..................... 44

Broccoli Salad 47

Vegetable Slaw with Blue Cheese Dressing 50

Macaroni Egg Salad 53

Fish, Eggplant, Mushroom Couscous Salad 56

Taco Salad 59

Detox Salad 63

Broccoli Salad with Bacon 66

Potato Curry Salad 69

Potato Bean Salad 72

German-style Potato Salad 75

Classic Potato Salad 78

Autumn Salad 81

Green Salad with Grilled Salmon 84

Pizza Salad 87

Spinach Salad with Deli Turkey 90

Salad with Pears and Pork 93

Tuna Pasta Salad 96

Southwestern Salad.. 99

Pasta Salad with Spinach Cilantro dressing...................... 102

Pasta Salad with Tomato Basil.. 106

Zoodle Pasta.. 109

Carrot Salad 112

Kale Salad with Apple Carrot Sticks 115

Corn, Avocado Raspberry Salad 118

Black Beans, Corn Mango Salad..................................... 121

Green Bean Salad 124

Egg Salad.. 127

Egg Vegetable Salad.. 130

Green Apple, Grapes Cabbage Salad............................... 133

Shrimp Cobb Salad 136

Turkey Salad 139

Cobb Salad in Mason Jar.. 143

Fruit Salad.. 147

Fruits in Honey Balsamic Dressing 150

Orange-Colored Fruit Salad 152

Tomato Plum Kimchi Salad 155

Avocado Pineapple Salad 159

Grape Salad with Walnuts 162

Conclusion 165

About the Author 166

Author's Afterthoughts 168

Introduction

Turning over a healthier leaf?

A healthier lifestyle starts with one's diet.

Including more fruits and vegetables in your diet is one of the first things that nutrition experts would recommend you do.

And eating salad is the most convenient way to do this.

Preparing salad usually only takes a few minutes. Just dice and slice, chop and shred, toss and mix, and that's it, you have crunchy delicious salad that you'd want to devour immediately.

That's not all. Salads are also versatile dishes that can be prepared in hundred different ways.

There are the fresh green salads made of lettuce or other leafy greens (spinach, arugula and so on), egg salads, bean salads, chicken salads, potato salads, fruit salads and many more.

Each of these salad types can be prepared in numerous ways. For example, you can add grilled salmon on your green salad, replace mayo with yogurt for your egg salad, or steam instead of boiling your potatoes for your potato salad.

This means that you'll never run out of options to serve.

Of course, we can't forget about the amazing benefits of salads to your health.

Eating salad means packing in more fiber, vitamins, minerals and antioxidants.

A high-fiber diet can boost your digestive health as well as lower cholesterol levels. Vitamins and minerals are necessary for optimal health. Antioxidants can keep numerous ailments at bay by neutralizing the harmful effects of free radicals in the body.

Experts have long established the positive effects of salad in one's health.

It's about time that you start enjoying these benefits. This recipe book is a good way to get started.

Caesar Pasta Salad

This is pasta and Caesar salad rolled into one with added bonus of chicken strips for one unforgettable salad dish. You can prepare this in 30 minutes or less. You can even make the dressing ahead to save time.

Serving size: 6

Preparation Cooking Time: 30 minutes

Ingredients:

- 1 cup Parmesan cheese, grated and divided
- 2 tablespoons freshly squeezed lemon juice
- 3 tablespoons olive oil
- 1 clove garlic, chopped
- ¼ cup reduced-fat plain yogurt
- ½ cup nonfat milk
- 1½ teaspoons anchovy paste
- 2 teaspoons Dijon mustard
- Salt and pepper to taste
- 4 cups cooked penne pasta
- 5 cups Romaine lettuce, chopped coarsely
- 1 cup cherry tomatoes, sliced in half
- 3 cups chicken breast fillet, cooked and shredded

Instructions:

1. Add half of the Parmesan cheese to a blender.

2. Pour in the lemon juice and olive oil.

3. Add the garlic, yogurt, milk, anchovy paste, mustard, salt and pepper.

4. Pulse until smooth. Set aside.

5. Toss the lettuce and cooked pasta in a large salad bowl.

6. Top with the tomatoes and shredded chicken.

7. Serve the salad with dressing and sprinkle the remaining Parmesan cheese on top.

Nutrients per Serving:

- Calories 383
- Fat 14 g
- Saturated fat 4 g
- Carbohydrates 34 g
- Fiber 4 g
- Protein 33 g
- Cholesterol 72 mg
- Sugars 4 g
- Sodium 572 mg
- Potassium 508 mg

Chicken Kale Salad

Here's a twist to your favorite chicken salad recipe. Instead of using lettuce, we will use fresh chopped kale. Instead of simply sprinkling the salad with Parmesan cheese, we will bake the cheese for an extra-special salad topping.

Serving size: 4

Preparation Cooking Time: 40 minutes

Ingredients:

- 1 cup Parmesan cheese, grated
- 1 lb. chicken breast fillet, cooked and shredded
- 2 cloves garlic
- Salt and pepper to taste
- 3 tablespoons freshly squeezed lemon juice
- ½ cup olive oil
- ½ teaspoon anchovy paste
- 1 tablespoon low-sodium tamari
- 11 cups kale, chopped
- 1 cup cherry tomatoes, sliced in half

Instructions:

1. Preheat your oven to 350 degrees F.

2. Cover your baking pan with parchment paper.

3. On the baking pan, create circles with the grated Parmesan cheese.

4. Bake for 13 minutes. Let cool.

5. Mash the garlic to form a paste.

6. Season with the salt.

7. Put the garlic in a bowl.

8. Stir in the lemon juice, oil, anchovy paste and tamari.

9. Massage the kale with this mixture.

10. Top with the crispy Parmesan rounds and tomatoes.

Nutrients per Serving:

- Calories 394
- Fat 26 g
- Saturated fat 6 g
- Carbohydrates 8 g
- Fiber 3 g
- Protein 32 g
- Cholesterol 75 mg
- Sugars 3 g
- Sodium 759 mg
- Potassium 570 mg

Apple Spinach Salad with Chicken Strips

A salad dish that's bound to impress your family and friends! You probably haven't tried combining apple and spinach before but as it turns out, they blend perfectly. Top it with chicken to round up the flavors.

Serving size: 4

Preparation Cooking Time: 20 minutes

Ingredients:

- ¼ cup Parmesan cheese, grated
- 2 tablespoons olive oil
- 3 tablespoons low-fat buttermilk
- 2 tablespoons honey
- 1 tablespoon cider vinegar
- 1 teaspoon poppy seeds
- ½ teaspoon Dijon mustard
- 1 tablespoon fresh thyme
- Salt to taste
- 5 cups baby spinach
- 1 apple, sliced thinly
- 1 cup chicken breast fillet, cooked and shredded

Instructions:

1. Combine the Parmesan cheese, oil, buttermilk, honey, vinegar, poppy seeds, mustard, thyme and salt.

2. Mix well.

3. Arrange the spinach in a salad bowl.

4. Top with the apple and chicken breast fillet shreds.

5. Serve the salad with the buttermilk dressing.

Nutrients per Serving:

- Calories 349
- Fat 17 g
- Saturated fat 4 g
- Carbohydrates 26 g
- Fiber 3 g
- Protein 23 g
- Cholesterol 50 mg
- Sugars 14 g
- Sodium 567 mg
- Potassium 249 mg

Asian Chicken Salad

You love chicken salad, but sometimes, you want it to taste a little bit different. Here's how to do it. Take it a notch higher by infusing it with Asian flavors. In this chicken salad, you'll be drizzling it with sesame pineapple dressing that you'd surely love.

Serving size: 6

Preparation Cooking Time: 20 minutes

Ingredients:

- 3 tablespoons olive oil
- ¼ cup rice vinegar
- ¼ cup pineapple juice
- 1 tablespoon low-sodium tamari
- 1½ teaspoons toasted sesame oil
- 2 teaspoons sugar
- Pepper to taste
- 4 chicken breast fillets
- 3 tablespoons low-sodium soy sauce
- 2 teaspoons ginger, grated
- 5 cups lettuce
- 1 cup red cabbage, chopped
- 1 cup cucumber sliced
- 1 cup carrot, shredded
- ¼ cup chopped green onions
- Toasted sesame seeds

Instructions:

1. Make the dressing by combining olive oil, vinegar, juice, tamari, sesame oil, sugar and pepper in a glass jar with lid.

2. Shake to blend well.

3. Preheat your broiler.

4. Broil the chicken for 5 minutes per side, brushing each side with the mixture of ginger and soy sauce.

5. Slice the chicken into strips.

6. Toss the lettuce, cabbage, cucumber and carrots in a salad bowl.

7. Top with the chicken strips.

8. Drizzle the dressing over the salad.

9. Garnish with the green onions and sesame seeds.

Nutrients per Serving:

- Calories 211
- Fat 10 g
- Saturated fat 2 g
- Carbohydrates 10 g
- Fiber 2 g
- Protein 20 g
- Cholesterol 44 mg
- Sugars 7 g
- Sodium 439 mg
- Potassium 281 mg

Chicken Salad with Brussels Sprouts Mushroom

Make your chicken salad a little bit different by using Brussels sprouts and mushrooms. Drizzle with Parmesan cheese dressing for the ultimate treat.

Serving size: 4

Preparation Cooking Time: 10 minutes

Ingredients:

- 3 tablespoons red wine vinegar
- 6 tablespoons olive oil
- 1 tablespoon Dijon mustard
- 2 teaspoons fresh thyme, chopped
- 1½ tablespoons green onion, minced
- Pepper to taste
- 4 cup arugula
- 4 cups Brussels sprouts, chopped
- 4 cups mushrooms, sliced
- 1 cup celery, sliced thinly
- 12 oz. chicken breast fillet, cooked and shredded
- 1 cup Parmesan cheese, shaved

Instructions:

1. Mix the vinegar, oil, mustard, thyme, green onion and pepper in a bowl.

2. Toss the arugula, Brussels sprouts, mushrooms and celery in the dressing.

3. Top with the chicken and Parmesan cheese.

Nutrients per Serving:

- Calories 432
- Fat 31 g
- Saturated fat 7 g
- Carbohydrates 15 g
- Fiber 5 g
- Protein 24 g
- Cholesterol 56 mg
- Sugars 6 g
- Sodium 533 mg
- Potassium 917 mg

Caesar Salad with Tofu

This Caesar salad is extra special because it is topped with crispy tofu croutons and drizzled with lemon mustard dressing.

Serving size: 10

Preparation Cooking Time: 35 minutes

Ingredients:

Tofu Croutons

- 8 oz. firm tofu, sliced into cubes
- 1 tablespoon oil
- Salad Dressing
- 2 tablespoons lemon juice
- 3 cloves garlic, sliced in half
- 1 teaspoon Dijon mustard
- 1 tablespoon water
- Salt and pepper to taste
- ¼ cup silken tofu
- ¼ cup soybean cooking oil

Salad

- 2 cups tomatoes, sliced
- 10 cups Romaine lettuce, torn
- ¼ cup Parmesan cheese, grated
- ¼ cup Kalamata olives, pitted and sliced

Instructions:

1. In a pan over medium heat, pour the oil and cook the tofu cubes until golden and crispy.

2. Drain on a plate covered with paper towel.

3. Make the dressing by adding all the dressing ingredients in a blender.

4. Process until smooth.

5. Toss the lettuce, tomatoes and olives in a salad bowl. Sprinkle the cheese on top.

6. Coat with the dressing and serve.

Nutrients per Serving:

- Calories 122
- Fat 10 g
- Saturated fat 2 g
- Carbohydrates 5 g
- Fiber 2 g
- Protein 5 g
- Cholesterol 1 mg
- Sugars 2 g
- Sodium 124 mg
- Potassium 240 mg

Beet Salad

Have you tried eating beet salad before? If not, it's about time that you do. You'll love the sweet and creamy flavor of beets. You can also use pre-cooked beets if you want to save time and effort.

Serving size: 6

Preparation Cooking Time: 1 hour and 10 minutes

Ingredients:

- 2 lb. beets
- 3 tablespoons olive oil
- 2 tablespoons balsamic vinegar
- Salt and pepper to taste
- ¼ cup feta cheese, crumbled
- 2 tablespoons fresh dill, chopped

Instructions:

1. Preheat your oven to 400 degrees F.

2. Wrap each beet with foil.

3. Put it on a baking pan and bake for 1 hour.

4. Let cool and slice into cubes.

5. Mix the oil, vinegar, salt and pepper in a salad bowl.

6. Toss the beets in the mixture.

7. Stir in the feta cheese and dill.

Nutrients per Serving:

- Calories 155
- Fat 9 g
- Saturated fat 2 g
- Carbohydrates 16 g
- Fiber 4 g
- Protein 4 g
- Cholesterol 7 mg
- Sugars 11 g
- Sodium 292 mg
- Potassium 505 mg

Fresh Green Salad

It doesn't get any simpler than this. With this fresh green salad, you'll be done with your preps within a few minutes. But just because it's quick and easy, it doesn't mean that it lacks in flavor and impact. You'll surely enjoy this salad recipe drizzled with herbed balsamic vinaigrette.

Serving size: 14

Preparation Cooking Time: 30 minutes

Ingredients:

- ¼ cup extra-virgin olive oil
- 2 cloves garlic, sliced
- 2 tablespoons fresh oregano
- ¼ cup balsamic vinegar
- Pepper to taste
- 16 cups mixed salad greens
- 4 tomatoes, sliced
- 1 cucumber, sliced
- 1 cup Kalamata olives, pitted
- ¼ cup fresh chives, chopped

Instructions:

1. Mix the oil, garlic, oregano, vinegar and pepper in a blender.

2. Pulse until smooth.

3. In a bowl, combine the salad greens, tomatoes, cucumbers and olives.

4. Drizzle the vinaigrette over the salad.

5. Sprinkle the chives on top.

Nutrients per Serving:

- Calories 76
- Fat 6 g
- Saturated fat 1 g
- Carbohydrates 5 g
- Fiber 1 g
- Protein 1g
- Cholesterol 0 mg
- Sugars 3 g
- Sodium 86 mg
- Potassium 149 mg

Greek Salad

If you don't have lettuce, but you want to make salad, why don't you give this Greek salad a try? This one consists only of cucumber, tomatoes, onion, bell pepper and olives. It is also topped with your favorite feta cheese. Serve it with crusty bread to complete the meal.

Serving size: 4

Preparation Cooking Time: 20 minutes

Ingredients:

- 1 ½ cups cucumber, diced
- ¼ cup onion, sliced thinly
- 2 tomatoes, diced
- 1 cup green bell pepper, diced
- ¼ cup Kalamata olives, pitted and sliced into quarters
- ½ cup feta cheese, diced
- 1 tablespoon freshly squeezed lemon juice
- 1 tablespoon red-wine vinegar
- 3 tablespoons olive oil
- 1 teaspoon dried oregano
- Salt and pepper to taste

Instructions:

1. Toss the cucumber, onion, tomatoes, green bell pepper, olives and feta in a salad bowl.

2. In another bowl, mix the lemon juice, vinegar, oil, oregano, salt and pepper.

3. Drizzle the salad with this dressing.

Nutrients per Serving:

- Calories 189
- Fat 16 g
- Saturated fat 4 g
- Carbohydrates 8 g
- Fiber 2 g
- Protein 4 g
- Cholesterol 17 mg
- Sugars 4 g
- Sodium 422 mg
- Potassium 311 mg

Cranberry Salad

The rich color is more than enough to entice you. When you get a taste of this healthy cranberry salad, you'd surely be delighted with how the berries, oranges, apples and celery blend perfectly together.

Serving size: 6

Preparation Cooking Time: 4 hours and 30 minutes

Ingredients:

- 1 lb. cranberries
- ¼ cup water
- ½ cup maple syrup
- 2 cup apples, chopped
- 1 cup orange, sliced into segments
- ½ cup celery, sliced thinly
- ½ cup walnuts, toasted and chopped
- 1 teaspoon lemon zest
- Salt to taste

Instructions:

1. Boil the cranberries in a mixture of water and maple syrup in a pot.

2. Reduce the heat and simmer for 15 minutes.

3. Remove from the stove. Let cool for half an hour.

4. Add the rest of the ingredients to the cranberry.

5. Refrigerate for 4 hours before serving.

Nutrients per Serving:

- Calories 202
- Fat 7 g
- Saturated fat 1 g
- Carbohydrates 37 g
- Fiber 5 g
- Protein 2 g
- Cholesterol 0 mg
- Sugars 26 g
- Sodium 210 mg
- Potassium 278 mg

Orange Raspberry Salad

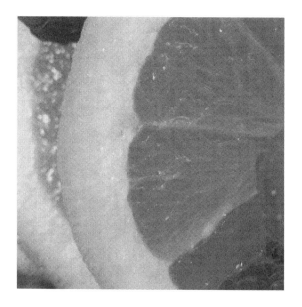

This salad certainly looks bright and cheery. But it's more than just an eye candy. It's also bursting with citrusy flavors, as well as loaded with vitamin C and many other nutrients. It definitely deserves a spot in your weekly menu.

Serving size: 6

Preparation Cooking Time: 15 minutes

Ingredients:

- 3 cups lettuce
- 3 cups baby spinach
- 10 oz. orange, sliced into segments
- 1 cup fresh raspberries
- 1 tablespoon freshly squeezed orange juice
- 1 tablespoon olive oil
- 1 tablespoon red-wine vinegar
- ¼ teaspoon dry mustard
- 1 teaspoon sugar
- ¼ cup almonds, toasted and slivered

Instructions:

1. Toss the lettuce, spinach, orange and raspberries in a salad bowl.

2. In a glass jar with lid, add the orange juice, olive oil, vinegar, mustard and sugar.

3. Drizzle the salad with the dressing.

4. Top with the slivered almonds.

Nutrients per Serving:

- Calories 89
- Fat 5 g
- Saturated fat 1 g
- Carbohydrates 10 g
- Fiber 2 g
- Protein 2 g
- Cholesterol 0 mg
- Sugars 7 g
- Sodium 10 mg
- Potassium 258 mg

Avocado Salad with Lime Cilantro Dressing

You're going to love this salad which is simply a combination of avocado and tomatoes, drizzled with dressing made with lime juice and cilantro.

Serving size: 6

Preparation Cooking Time: 30 minutes

Ingredients:

- 2 cups baby spinach
- 2 avocados, sliced
- 6 tomatoes, sliced
- 3 tablespoons extra-virgin olive oil
- ¼ cup lime juice
- 3 tablespoons fresh cilantro, chopped
- 1 teaspoon lime zest
- Salt and pepper to taste

Instructions:

1. Arrange the baby spinach in a salad bowl.

2. Top with the avocado and tomatoes.

3. Combine the rest of the ingredients in another bowl to make the dressing.

4. Pour the dressing on top of the salad.

Nutrients per Serving:

- Calories 130
- Fat 12 g
- Saturated fat 2 g
- Carbohydrates 7 g
- Fiber 3 g
- Protein 2 g
- Cholesterol 0 mg
- Sugars 2 g
- Sodium 115 mg
- Potassium 361 mg

Broccoli Salad

Here's a quick and simple broccoli salad that's made extra special with the addition of onions, Parmesan cheese and toasted pecans.

Serving size: 6

Preparation Cooking Time: 30 minutes

Ingredients:

- 8 cups broccoli florets
- ¼ cup olive oil
- 2 tablespoons red wine vinegar
- 1 teaspoon mustard
- 1 teaspoon honey
- 2 teaspoons fresh thyme, chopped
- Salt to taste
- ½ cup onion, sliced
- ½ cup Parmesan cheese, shaved
- ¼ cup pecans, toasted and chopped

Instructions:

1. Fill a pot with water.

2. Place a steamer basket inside.

3. Steam the broccoli for 4 minutes.

4. Transfer the broccoli to a bowl and fill with ice.

5. Pat the broccoli dry using paper towels.

6. In a glass jar with lid, combine the oil, vinegar, mustard, honey, thyme and salt.

7. Toss the broccoli in onion and dressing.

8. Top with the cheese and pecans before serving.

Nutrients per Serving:

- Calories 199
- Fat 17 g
- Saturated fat 3 g
- Carbohydrates 8 g
- Fiber 3 g
- Protein 5 g
- Cholesterol 3 mg
- Sugars 3 g
- Sodium 366 mg
- Potassium 349 mg

Vegetable Slaw with Blue Cheese Dressing

Most people make veggie slaw by tossing shredded cabbage and carrot strips in mayo. But here's a better way to do it: mix it with blue cheese and buttermilk. Pair it with grilled fish or barbecue pork.

Serving size: 6

Preparation Cooking Time: 15 minutes

Ingredients:

- 2 tablespoons cider vinegar
- ¼ cup mayonnaise
- ¼ cup buttermilk
- ½ cup blue cheese, crumbled
- ¼ cup parsley, chopped
- 4 cups cabbage, chopped
- 1 cup carrot, shredded
- 1 ½ cups red and green bell pepper, sliced into strips
- ¼ cup sunflower seeds, toasted

Instructions:

1. Combine the vinegar, mayo, buttermilk, blue cheese and parsley in a bowl.

2. Mix well.

3. Toss the cabbage, carrot, red bell pepper and green bell pepper in the blue cheese dressing.

4. Top with the sunflower seeds.

Nutrients per Serving:

- Calories 166
- Fat 13 g
- Saturated fat 4 g
- Carbohydrates 8 g
- Fiber 3 g
- Protein 5 g
- Cholesterol 13 mg
- Sugars 4 g
- Sodium 260 mg
- Potassium 267 mg

Macaroni Egg Salad

Take the classic macaroni salad and combine it with deviled eggs. You'll end up with a crowd-pleasing salad dish that would be a huge hit wherever you bring it.

Serving size: 8

Preparation Cooking Time: 30 minutes

Ingredients:

- 8 cups cooked macaroni pasta
- 1 avocado
- 5 hardboiled eggs
- ¼ cup mayonnaise
- 2 tablespoons freshly squeezed lemon juice
- 3 tablespoons Greek yogurt
- 1 cup scallions, sliced
- 1 tablespoon Dijon mustard
- ½ cup celery, chopped
- ¼ cup dill, chopped
- Salt and pepper to taste

Instructions:

1. Place the macaronic pasta in a large salad bowl. Set aside.

2. In another bowl, mash the avocado and eggs.

3. Stir in the rest of the ingredients.

4. Transfer the egg mixture to the pasta.

5. Mix well.

6. Chill before serving.

Nutrients per Serving:

- Calories 224
- Fat 11 g
- Saturated fat 2 g
- Carbohydrates 23 g
- Fiber 3 g
- Protein 9 g
- Cholesterol 120 mg
- Sugars 2 g
- Sodium 307 mg
- Potassium 166 mg

Fish, Eggplant, Mushroom Couscous Salad

If you have leftover fish like salmon, you can use it to make this incredible salad. Combine baby spinach, eggplant, mushrooms and fish flakes, and that's it! It only takes a few minutes to prepare.

Serving size: 1

Preparation Cooking Time: 10 minutes

Ingredients:

- Cooking spray
- ¼ cup eggplant, diced
- ¼ cup mushrooms, sliced
- 3 cups baby spinach
- 2 tablespoon vinaigrette
- ¼ cup whole wheat couscous, cooked
- 4 oz. cooked salmon or any fish fillet
- ¼ cup dried apricots, sliced
- 2 tablespoons goat cheese, crumbled

Instructions:

1. Spray your pan with oil.

2. Place it over medium heat.

3. Cook the eggplant and mushrooms for 4 minutes, stirring frequently.

4. Transfer to a plate.

5. In a salad bowl, toss the spinach and couscous with vinaigrette.

6. Top with the fish flakes, eggplant, mushrooms and the rest of the ingredients.

Nutrients per Serving:

- Calories 464
- Fat 22 g
- Saturated fat 5 g
- Carbohydrates 35 g
- Fiber 6 g
- Protein 35 g
- Cholesterol 69 mg
- Sugars 19 g
- Sodium 352 mg
- Potassium 1489 mg

Taco Salad

You and your family are going to love this taco salad. But what makes this one stand out from other taco salads is that this one comes with lentils. Don't worry about taking too long with the preparation. You can prepare the lentils in your slow cooker and simply wait for these to be cooked.

Serving size: 8

Preparation Cooking Time: 10 hours and 40 minutes

Ingredients:

- 1 cup onion, chopped
- 3 cloves garlic, crushed and minced
- 1 cup red bell pepper, chopped
- 1 cup green bell pepper, chopped
- 1 cup dry lentils, rinsed and drained
- ½ cup brown rice (uncooked)
- Salt to taste
- 2 teaspoons chili powder
- 28 oz. low-sodium chicken stock
- 1 cup summer squash, sliced
- 3 cups baby spinach
- 3 cups lettuce
- 2 cups tortilla chips
- ½ cup cheddar cheese, grated
- 1 cup Greek yogurt
- 2 cups tomatoes, chopped

Instructions:

1. Add the onion, garlic, bell peppers, lentils, rice, salt, chili powder and chicken stock in a slow cooker.

2. Mix well.

3. Cover the pot.

4. Cook on low for 10 hours.

5. Set the slow cooker to high.

6. Add the squash.

7. Seal and cook for another 20 minutes.

8. Add the lettuce and spinach in a bowl.

9. Spread the lentil mixture on top.

10. Top with the tortilla, cheddar, yogurt and tomatoes.

Nutrients per Serving:

- Calories 262
- Fat 6 g
- Saturated fat 1 g
- Carbohydrates 40 g
- Fiber 11 g
- Protein 15 g
- Cholesterol 5 mg
- Sugars 7 g
- Sodium 446 mg
- Potassium 588 mg

Detox Salad

Here's a salad that's perfect for you when you feel like you need a good cleansing and detox.

Serving size: 4

Preparation Cooking Time: 50 minutes

Ingredients:

- 3 cups butternut squash, cubed
- 1 tablespoon olive oil
- Salt and pepper to taste
- ¼ teaspoon cumin
- ¼ teaspoon turmeric
- ¼ cup apple cider vinegar
- ¼ cup extra virgin olive oil
- 1 tablespoon pure maple syrup
- 2 tablespoons low-fat Greek yogurt
- 1 shallot, chopped
- 1 cup kale, chopped
- 1 pint Brussels sprouts, slivered
- 1 tablespoon pumpkin seeds
- 1 avocado, cubed

Instructions:

1. Preheat your oven to 425 degrees F.

2. Arrange the squash in a single layer on a baking pan.

3. Drizzle with oil and season with salt, pepper, cumin and turmeric.

4. Roast in the oven for 15 minutes.

5. Stir and roast for another 10 minutes.

6. In a glass jar, mix the vinegar, extra virgin olive oil, maple syrup, yogurt and shallot.

7. Shake to blend well.

8. Toss the rest of the ingredients in a large salad bowl.

9. Stir in the roasted squash and pour the dressing over the salad.

Nutrients per Serving:

- Calories 377
- Fat 28 g
- Saturated fat 4 g
- Carbohydrates 25 g
- Fiber 8 g
- Protein 9 g
- Cholesterol 0 mg
- Sugars 8 g
- Sodium 124 mg
- Potassium 1079 mg

Broccoli Salad with Bacon

Inviting friends over but have no idea what to prepare for them? Here's an option that you'd surely want to consider: broccoli salad with cranberries and water chestnuts, sprinkled with crispy bacon bits on top.

Serving size: 6

Preparation Cooking Time: 20 minutes

Ingredients:

- 2 teaspoons cider vinegar
- ¼ cup reduced-fat mayonnaise
- ¼ cup low-fat sour cream
- 1 clove garlic, crushed and minced
- 1 teaspoon sugar
- 4 cups broccoli florets, chopped
- 8 oz. water chestnuts, chopped
- 3 slices bacon, cooked and crumbled
- 3 tablespoons dried cranberries
- Pepper to taste

Instructions:

1. Add the vinegar, mayonnaise, sour cream, garlic and sugar in a glass jar with lid.

2. Shake to blend well.

3. Toss the broccoli with the rest of the ingredients in a salad bowl.

4. Coat evenly with the dressing.

Nutrients per Serving:

- Calories 92
- Fat 5 g
- Saturated fat 2 g
- Carbohydrates 11 g
- Fiber 2 g
- Protein 3 g
- Cholesterol 10 mg
- Sugars 4 g
- Sodium 160 mg
- Potassium 191 mg

Potato Curry Salad

This is a different take on your favorite potato salad. It makes use of yogurt instead of just mayonnaise, and you don't have to peel the potatoes to pack it with more protein and fiber.

Serving size: 10

Preparation Cooking Time: 40 minutes

Ingredients:

- 3 lb. potatoes, diced
- Salt and pepper to taste
- ½ cup mayonnaise
- ½ cup reduced-fat plain yogurt
- 2 onions, chopped
- 2 tablespoons Dijon mustard
- 2 teaspoons curry powder
- 1 red bell pepper, chopped
- ½ cup green peas

Instructions:

1. Fill your pot with water and place a steamer basket inside.

2. Steam the potatoes for 15 minutes.

3. Transfer to a baking pan and season with salt.

4. Let sit for 20 minutes.

5. While waiting, mix the rest of the ingredients except the peas and bell pepper.

6. Blend well.

7. Toss the potatoes with the bell pepper and peas.

8. Coat evenly with the mayo and yogurt mixture.

Nutrients per Serving:

- Calories 141
- Fat 3 g
- Saturated fat 1 g
- Carbohydrates 26 g
- Fiber 2 g
- Protein 4 g
- Cholesterol 3 mg
- Sugars 4 g
- Sodium 316 mg
- Potassium 557 mg

Potato Bean Salad

This is one potato salad you surely won't get enough of. In this recipe, you add green beans to the mix and make the salad more palatable with bacon and blue cheese. Make use of red or yellow potatoes, which are most suitable for potato salads. If you're not fond of moldy cheese, swap it with feta or goat cheese.

Serving size: 10

Preparation Cooking Time: 1 hour and 10 minutes

Ingredients:

- 2 lb. potatoes, diced
- Salt and pepper to taste
- 3 tablespoons white wine vinegar
- 1 tablespoon Dijon mustard
- ¼ cup olive oil
- ¼ cup shallot, chopped
- 2 cups green beans, cooked, trimmed and sliced
- 3 slices bacon, cooked and minced
- ¼ cup blue cheese, crumbled

Instructions:

1. Fill your pot with water.

2. Add a steamer basket inside.

3. Steam the potatoes for 15 minutes or until tender.

4. Arrange the potatoes on a baking pan and season with salt.

5. Let sit for 20 minutes.

6. While waiting, combine the vinegar, mustard, oil, pepper and shallot.

7. Toss the potatoes and green beans in a salad bowl.

8. Top with the bacon and blue cheese.

9. Pour the sauce over the salad and mix well.

10. Refrigerate for 30 minutes before serving.

Nutrients per Serving:

- Calories 174
- Fat 8 g
- Saturated fat 2 g
- Carbohydrates 23 g
- Fiber 2 g
- Protein 4 g
- Cholesterol 5 mg
- Sugars 1 g
- Sodium 280 mg
- Potassium 534 mg

German-style Potato Salad

There are two things that make this potato salad different from other recipes. One, the potatoes are simmered for long hours in the slow cooker instead of boiled or steamed. Two, the dressing is not made with mayonnaise. Try it, there's a big chance you'll love this recipe.

Serving size: 16

Preparation Cooking Time: 5 hours and 20 minutes

Ingredients:

- 4 slices bacon
- ¼ cup cider vinegar
- 2 tablespoons all-purpose flour
- 3 tablespoons mustard
- Salt and pepper to taste
- 1 onion, chopped
- 2 cups celery, sliced
- 3 lb. potatoes, diced
- ¼ cup fresh dill, chopped

Instructions:

1. In a pan over medium heat, cook the bacon until golden and crispy.

2. Drain on a plate lined with paper towel.

3. Chop into smaller pieces.

4. Pour the vinegar into the same pan to deglaze.

5. Scrape browned bits with wooden spoon.

6. In a bowl, mix the flour, mustard and vinegar with bacon browned bits.

7. Season with the salt and pepper.

8. Add the onion, celery and potatoes into your slow cooker.

9. Pour in the vinegar mixture.

10. Toss to coat evenly.

11. Seal the pot and cook on low setting for 5 hours.

12. Top with the bacon bits and serve with the dill.

Nutrients per Serving:

- Calories 91
- Fat 1 g
- Saturated fat 0 g
- Carbohydrates 17 g
- Fiber 1 g
- Protein 3 g
- Cholesterol 2 mg
- Sugars 1 g
- Sodium 172 mg
- Potassium 415 mg

Classic Potato Salad

Of course, the classic recipe is still hard to beat. There will always be those times when you'll crave for the simple and easy potato salad recipe you've grown to love. Don't peel the potatoes for extra potassium and fiber.

Serving size: 10

Preparation Cooking Time: 45 minutes

Ingredients:

- 2 lb. potatoes, diced
- Salt and pepper to taste
- ½ cup reduced-fat yogurt
- ½ cup light mayonnaise
- 2 tablespoons Dijon mustard
- ¼ onion, chopped
- 2 hard-boiled eggs, sliced into smaller pieces
- 1 cup celery, chopped

Instructions:

1. Fill a pot or saucepan with water.

2. Add the steamer basket inside.

3. Steam the potatoes for 15 minutes.

4. Let cool on a baking pan.

5. Sprinkle with the salt.

6. While waiting, mix the yogurt, mayo, mustard and onion.

7. Season with the salt and pepper.

8. Toss the potatoes, celery and eggs in a salad bowl.

9. Stir in the mayo mixture.

10. Chill in the refrigerator for at least 30 minutes before serving.

Nutrients per Serving:

- Calories 146
- Fat 4 g
- Saturated fat 1 g
- Carbohydrates 24 g
- Fiber 2 g
- Protein 5 g
- Cholesterol 40 mg
- Sugars 3 g
- Sodium 325 mg
- Potassium 552 mg

Autumn Salad

This salad showcases the vibrant colors of autumn. But it doesn't mean that you'd have to wait for fall before you can enjoy this recipe. You can make it anytime you want. It's a beautiful and delicious combination of apples, squash, spinach and cheese.

Serving size: 8

Preparation Cooking Time: 40 minutes

Ingredients:

- 4 cups butternut squash, diced
- 3 tablespoons olive oil, divided
- 2 cloves garlic, crushed and minced
- Salt and pepper to taste
- 2 teaspoons Dijon mustard
- 1 teaspoon maple syrup
- 2 tablespoons balsamic vinegar
- 8 cups baby spinach
- 1 apple, diced
- ½ cup pecans, toasted and chopped
- ½ cup cheddar cheese, diced

Instructions:

1. Toss the squash cubes in 1 tablespoon oil and garlic.

2. Season with the salt and pepper.

3. Add to a baking sheet and roast in the oven at 350 degrees F for 20 minutes or until tender.

4. While waiting, make the dressing by combining the mustard, maple syrup and vinegar.

5. Sprinkle with a little salt and pepper.

6. In a large bowl, combine the roasted squash with the apples, pecans and cheese.

7. Coat evenly with the mustard dressing.

Nutrients per Serving:

- Calories 185
- Fat 12 g
- Saturated fat 3 g
- Carbohydrates 16 g
- Fiber 4 g
- Protein 5 g
- Cholesterol 7 mg
- Sugars 5 g
- Sodium 255 mg
- Potassium 315 mg

Green Salad with Grilled Salmon

You're going to fall in love with this fresh garden salad topped with succulent herbed salmon. Making this salad even more enticing are the crumbled feta cheese and chopped pistachios.

Serving size: 4

Preparation Cooking Time: 30 minutes

Ingredients:

- 4 salmon fillets (skinless)
- 1 tablespoons garlic and herb seasoning
- Salt and pepper to taste
- 1 onion, chopped
- 6 cups Romaine lettuce, chopped
- 2 cucumbers, sliced into rounds
- 2 cups cherry tomatoes, sliced in half
- 1 tablespoon fresh basil, chopped
- 1 tablespoon fresh dill, chopped
- 1 teaspoon Dijon mustard
- 2 tablespoon freshly squeezed lemon juice
- 3 tablespoons extra-virgin olive oil
- ¼ cup feta cheese, crumbled
- 2 tablespoons pistachios, chopped

Instructions:

1. Preheat your grill.

2. Season both sides of salmon with the garlic herb blend, salt and pepper.

3. Grill the salmon for 4 minutes per side.

4. In a bowl, toss the lettuce, cucumbers, tomatoes, dill and basil.

5. In a glass jar with lid, blend the mustard, lemon juice and olive oil. Shake.

6. Pour the dressing over the salad and mix well.

7. Top with the feta cheese, pistachios and grilled salmon.

Nutrients per Serving:

- Calories 418
- Fat 25 g
- Saturated fat 5 g
- Carbohydrates 10 g
- Fiber 4 g
- Protein 30 g
- Cholesterol 22 mg
- Sugars 1 g
- Sodium 450 mg
- Potassium 290 mg

Pizza Salad

Pizza is considered one of the unhealthiest foods. But what if you turn it into a salad? Now, you don't have any reason not to enjoy pizza!

Serving size: 6

Preparation Cooking Time: 35 minutes

Ingredients:

- 4 oz. ground turkey
- Garlic salt to taste
- 1 lb. whole-wheat pizza dough
- ½ cup crushed tomatoes
- 1 cup mozzarella cheese
- ½ cup feta cheese, crumbled
- 2 tablespoons olive oil
- 1 teaspoon honey
- 1 tablespoon lemon juice
- 3 cup lettuce, chopped
- 3 cups baby arugula

Instructions:

1. Preheat your oven to 425 degrees F.

2. Cover the top of your pizza pan with parchment paper. Set aside.

3. In a pan over medium heat, cook the ground turkey and season with garlic salt.

4. Cook for 5 minutes, stirring frequently to break it up.

5. Roll out the pizza dough on your pan.

6. Spread the tomatoes on top of the dough.

7. Sprinkle top with the two cheeses and ground turkey.

8. Bake for 15 minutes.

9. Mix the oil, honey and lemon juice.

10. Toss the lettuce and arugula in this mixture.

11. Top the pizza with the salad.

Nutrients per Serving:

- Calories 339
- Fat 17 g
- Saturated fat 5 g
- Carbohydrates 35 g
- Fiber 2 g
- Protein 16 g
- Cholesterol 34 mg
- Sugars 5 g
- Sodium 603 mg
- Potassium 202 mg

Spinach Salad with Deli Turkey

It's pretty impressive how all the flavors of the goat cheese, turkey slices, blueberries, beets and onions blend perfectly in this simple but refreshing spinach salad.

Serving size: 1

Preparation Cooking Time: 15 minutes

Ingredients:

- 2 cups baby spinach
- 2 tablespoons onion, sliced thinly
- ¼ cup fresh blueberries
- 2 tablespoons goat cheese, crumbled
- ½ cup beets, sliced thinly
- 1 oz. turkey deli slices
- 2 teaspoons extra-virgin olive oil
- 1 tablespoon balsamic vinegar
- 1 tablespoon orange juice

Instructions:

1. Arrange the spinach on a plate.

2. Sprinkle the onion, blueberries and cheese on top.

3. Add the beets and turkey slices.

4. Make the dressing by mixing the rest of the ingredients.

5. Drizzle on top of the salad.

Nutrients per Serving:

- Calories 262
- Fat 13 g
- Saturated fat 3 g
- Carbohydrates 23 g
- Fiber 4 g
- Protein 15 g
- Cholesterol 29 mg
- Sugars 17 g
- Sodium 383 mg
- Potassium 560 mg

Salad with Pears and Pork

Turn a dull night into an exciting one with this amazing salad made with arugula, pears and roasted pork tenderloin. This is simple enough that even if you're busy, you won't take long preparing this.

Serving size: 4

Preparation Cooking Time: 50 minutes

Ingredients:

- Cooking spray
- 2 tablespoons olive oil
- 1 clove garlic, crushed and minced
- 2 teaspoons freshly squeezed lemon juice
- 3 tablespoons balsamic vinegar
- 1 teaspoon Dijon mustard
- 1 teaspoon honey
- 2 teaspoons fresh rosemary, chopped
- Salt and pepper to taste
- 1 lb. pork tenderloin
- 4 pears, sliced thinly
- 8 cups arugula
- ¼ cup blue cheese, crumbled
- 2 tablespoons walnuts, toasted and chopped

Instructions:

1. Preheat your oven to 400 degrees F.

2. Spray your baking pan with oil.

3. In a pan over medium heat,

4. Combine the oil, garlic, juice, vinegar, mustard, honey, rosemary, salt and pepper in a bowl.

5. Mix well and set aside.

6. Put the pork on the baking pan.

7. Season both sides with the salt and pepper.

8. Take 2 tablespoons of the mustard mixture and brush on both sides of the pork.

9. Roast in the oven for 20 minutes.

10. Let cool before slicing.

11. Toss the pears and arugula in the dressing.

12. Add the roasted pork, cheese and toasted walnuts on top.

Nutrients per Serving:

- Calories 352
- Fat 16 g
- Saturated fat 4 g
- Carbohydrates 25 g
- Fiber 5 g
- Protein 27 g
- Cholesterol 62 mg
- Sugars 16 g
- Sodium 692 mg
- Potassium 982 mg

Tuna Pasta Salad

If you've never tried mixing tuna and pasta for salad, it's time that you do. This recipe is not only tasty and impressive, it's also healthy—packed with omega 3 and vitamins. The arugula, sun-dried tomatoes and zucchini make the salad even healthier and more delicious.

Serving size: 6

Preparation Cooking Time: 30 minutes

Ingredients:

Dressing

- ¼ cup low-sodium chicken broth
- ¼ cup in olive oil
- 2 tablespoons shallots, chopped
- 1 tablespoon dried basil
- ¼ cup red-wine vinegar
- Salt and pepper to taste

Salad

- 8 oz. whole-wheat fusilli
- 3 cups baby arugula
- 1 cup zucchini, diced
- 10 oz. canned tuna flakes
- ½ cup Parmesan cheese, shredded
- ¼ cup sun-dried tomatoes, chopped
- Pepper to taste

Instructions:

1. Add all the dressing ingredients in a glass jar with lid.

2. Shake to blend well.

3. Cook the pasta according to directions in the package.

4. Drain and let cool.

5. Toss with the rest of the salad ingredients.

6. Drizzle the dressing over the salad.

Nutrients per Serving:

- Calories 275
- Fat 12 g
- Saturated fat 3 g
- Carbohydrates 28 g
- Fiber 3 g
- Protein 15 g
- Cholesterol 17 mg
- Sugars 3 g
- Sodium 330 mg
- Potassium 335 mg

Southwestern Salad

When you think about salad, you think about lettuce and other leafy greens. Here's a different kind of salad that's also bursting with flavors and will give you just the same amount of satisfaction.

Serving size: 1

Preparation Cooking Time: 15 minutes

Ingredients:

- 1 tablespoon Greek yogurt
- 1 tablespoon salsa
- ¾ cup red bell pepper, chopped
- 1 cup tomatoes, chopped
- ½ cup whole-wheat orzo, cooked and cooled
- 2 cups edamame, cooked and cooled
- 1 onion, chopped
- 2 tablespoons Jack cheese, shredded
- Hot sauce
- Salt and pepper to taste

Instructions:

1. Mix the yogurt and salsa in a bowl.

2. Arrange the bell pepper, tomatoes, orzo, edamame and onion in a salad bowl.

3. Drizzle with the dressing, cheese and hot sauce.

4. Season with the salt and pepper.

Nutrients per Serving:

- Calories 403
- Fat 13 g
- Saturated fat 3 g
- Carbohydrates 51 g
- Fiber 15 g
- Protein 24 g
- Cholesterol 14 mg
- Sugars 14 g
- Sodium 520 mg
- Potassium 1229 mg

Pasta Salad with Spinach Cilantro dressing

This is another southwestern inspired salad that's made with pasta drizzled with spinach and cilantro dressing. To take it a notch higher, you add some almonds, cilantro and red pepper.

Serving size: 6

Preparation Cooking Time: 30 minutes

Ingredients:

Dressing

- 2 tablespoons water
- 1 tablespoon olive oil
- 1 cup spinach
- Salt and pepper to taste
- ¼ teaspoon red pepper flakes, crushed
- 2 tablespoons almonds, toasted and chopped
- ¼ cup sour cream

Salad

- 4 oz. penne pasta
- ½ cup red bell pepper, chopped
- ½ cup zucchini, sliced into strips
- ¼ cup radishes, sliced
- ¼ cup corn kernels

Instructions:

1. Add all the dressing ingredients except sour cream in a food processor.

2. Pulse until smooth.

3. Stir in the cream and pulse some more.

4. To prepare the salad, cook the pasta according to directions.

5. Let cool and add to a salad bowl.

6. Toss the pasta with the rest of the salad ingredients.

7. Coat with the spinach and cilantro dressing evenly.

8. Chill before serving.

Nutrients per Serving:

- Calories 130
- Fat 5 g
- Saturated fat 1 g
- Carbohydrates 18 g
- Fiber 3 g
- Protein 5 g
- Cholesterol 3 mg
- Sugars 1 g
- Sodium 219 mg
- Potassium 171 mg

Pasta Salad with Tomato Basil

Do you love tomato and basil pasta? For sure, you'll fall in love just as much with this pasta salad version. This is best served with grilled chicken or beef main course.

Serving size: 16

Preparation Cooking Time: 30 minutes

Ingredients:

- 1 lb. gemelli pasta
- 1 lb. tomatoes, chopped
- 1 cup mozzarella cheese
- ½ cup onion, sliced thinly
- ½ cup olives, pitted and sliced
- ¼ cup fresh basil, chopped
- 2 tablespoons fresh oregano, chopped
- 2 tablespoons capers
- 2 cloves garlic, crushed and minced
- Salt and pepper to taste
- 2 tablespoons olive oil

Instructions:

1. Cook the pasta according to the directions in the package.

2. Drain and let cool.

3. In a bowl, mix the rest of the ingredients together.

4. Stir in the pasta.

5. Cover with foil and chill in the refrigerator before serving.

Nutrients per Serving:

- Calories 152
- Fat 4 g
- Saturated fat 1 g
- Carbohydrates 23 g
- Fiber 1 g
- Protein 6 g
- Cholesterol 4 mg
- Sugars 2 g
- Sodium 161 mg
- Potassium 560 mg

Zoodle Pasta

Zucchini noodles is a popular vegan alternative to pasta. In this recipe, you use this as the main ingredient for your salad, made with tomatoes, olives and mustard dressing.

Serving size: 4

Preparation Cooking Time: 15 minutes

Ingredients:

- 5 tablespoons olive oil
- 1 clove garlic, grated
- 2 teaspoons Dijon mustard
- 3 tablespoons red-wine vinegar
- 1 stalk shallot, chopped
- 2 tablespoons fresh oregano, chopped
- 16 oz. zucchini noodles
- ¼ cup Kalamata olives, pitted
- 3 cups cherry tomatoes, sliced in half
- ¾ cup Parmesan cheese, shaved

Instructions:

1. Combine the oil, garlic, mustard, vinegar, shallot and oregano in a glass jar with lid.

2. Shake to blend well.

3. Toss the zucchini noodles with the olives and tomatoes.

4. Drizzle the salad dressing on top and mix.

5. Sprinkle the Parmesan cheese on top.

Nutrients per Serving:

- Calories 299
- Fat 25 g
- Saturated fat 5 g
- Carbohydrates 12 g
- Fiber 3 g
- Protein 7 g
- Cholesterol 13 mg
- Sugars 4 g
- Sodium 480 mg
- Potassium 627 mg

Carrot Salad

Super crunchy carrot salad with peanut flavored dressing—this is one unique salad that you would love to prepare for your family and friends.

Serving size: 4

Preparation Cooking Time: 15 minutes

Ingredients:

Dressing

- 1 tablespoon freshly squeezed lime juice
- 2 tablespoons peanut butter
- 2 tablespoons peanut oil
- 1 tablespoon water
- 1 tablespoon low-sodium tamari
- 1 tablespoon cilantro, chopped
- 1 tablespoon basil, chopped
- 1 lb. carrots, spiralized
- 1 tablespoon roasted peanuts, chopped

Instructions:

1. Dissolve the peanut butter in lime juice.

2. Toss these with the rest of the ingredients except the peanuts in a large bowl.

3. Sprinkle the peanuts on top before serving.

Nutrients per Serving:

- Calories 165
- Fat 12 g
- Saturated fat 2 g
- Carbohydrates 13 g
- Fiber 3 g
- Protein 4 g
- Cholesterol 0 mg
- Sugars 6 g
- Sodium 287 mg
- Potassium 391 mg

Kale Salad with Apple Carrot Sticks

This is one salad that will definitely make you feel good about yourself especially if you've been having more cheat days than allowed! It is a super healthy salad made with kale topped with apple and carrot sticks.

Serving size: 12

Preparation Cooking Time: 30 minutes

Ingredients:

Dressing

- ¼ cup cider vinegar
- 3 tablespoons olive oil
- 1 shallot, minced
- 2 tablespoons apple cider
- 2 teaspoons pure maple syrup
- 1 tablespoon mustard
- Salt and pepper to taste

Salad

- 10 cups kale
- 3 cups carrots, sliced into thin sticks
- 2 apples, sliced into thin sticks
- ¼ cup parsley, chopped
- 1 cup radish, sliced into thin sticks

Instructions:

1. Prepare the dressing by adding all the dressing ingredients in a blender.

2. Pulse until smooth.

3. Toss the salad ingredients in a bowl.

4. Pour the dressing on top and mix to coat evenly.

Nutrients per Serving:

- Calories 75
- Fat 4 g
- Saturated fat 1 g
- Carbohydrates 9 g
- Fiber 2 g
- Protein 1 g
- Cholesterol 0 mg
- Sugars 6 g
- Sodium 159 mg
- Potassium 212 mg

Corn, Avocado Raspberry Salad

The bright colors of this healthy salad will definitely entice you. Everything blends so well together and made even more appetizing with the lime dressing.

Serving size: 6

Preparation Cooking Time: 15 minutes

Ingredients:

- 3 tablespoons freshly squeezed lime juice
- 1 tablespoon extra-virgin olive oil
- Pinch cayenne pepper
- Salt to taste
- 2 cups corn kernels
- 1 cup fresh raspberries
- 1 avocado, cubed
- 4 radish, sliced thinly
- ¼ cup scallions, chopped

Instructions:

1. Mix the lime juice, olive oil, cayenne pepper and salt in a bowl.

2. In a salad bowl, combine the rest of the ingredients.

3. Stir in the lime dressing.

4. Coat evenly.

Nutrients per Serving:

- Calories 116
- Fat 7 g
- Saturated fat 1 g
- Carbohydrates 15 g
- Fiber 5 g
- Protein 2 g
- Cholesterol 0 mg
- Sugars 5 g
- Sodium 205 mg
- Potassium 311 mg

Black Beans, Corn Mango Salad

If you're looking for a salad to pair with your grilled dish, this is the perfect option. To achieve the best results, brown and caramelize the corn, as this blends perfectly with the sweet flavors of mango.

Serving size: 8

Preparation Cooking Time: 15 minutes

Ingredients:

- 2 teaspoons olive oil
- 1 clove garlic, crushed and minced
- 1 cup corn kernels
- 2 onions, chopped
- 2 red bell peppers, diced
- 15 oz. black beans, rinsed and drained
- 1 mango, diced
- 1 chipotle pepper in adobo sauce, chopped
- 3 tablespoons freshly squeezed lime juice
- $\frac{1}{4}$ teaspoon ground cumin
- 1 tablespoon cilantro, chopped
- Salt to taste

Instructions:

1. Pour the oil in a pan over medium heat.

2. Cook the garlic for 30 seconds.

3. Add the corn and cook while stirring for 5 minutes.

4. Transfer the corn and garlic in a bowl.

5. Stir in the rest of the ingredients and serve.

Nutrients per Serving:

- Calories 122
- Fat 2 g
- Saturated fat 0 g
- Carbohydrates 25 g
- Fiber 4 g
- Protein 4 g
- Cholesterol 0 mg
- Sugars 11 g
- Sodium 245 mg
- Potassium 230 mg

Green Bean Salad

There are many types of green bean salad but this is one of the easiest to prepare, and also one of the most unforgettable you'll ever try. For best results, blanch the green beans just long enough to cook them but at the same time, make sure they're still crunchy. The key is to soak them in ice water right after cooking.

Serving size: 8

Preparation Cooking Time: 45 minutes

Ingredients:

- 2 lb. green beans, trimmed and sliced
- 3 cups corn kernels
- 1 onion, minced
- ½ cup black olives, pitted and sliced in half
- 1 red bell pepper, minced
- ¼ cup olive oil
- 2 cloves garlic, crushed and minced
- 3 tablespoons freshly squeezed lemon juice
- 3 tablespoons balsamic vinegar
- ¼ cup fresh basil, chopped
- Salt and pepper to taste

Instructions:

1. Fill a pot with water and bring to a boil.

2. Fill another pot with ice water.

3. Soak the green beans in hot water for 2 to 3 minutes or until tender.

4. Drain and then soak in ice water. Let sit for 1 to 2 minutes.

5. Transfer to a salad bowl.

6. Stir in the corn and the rest of the ingredients.

Nutrients per Serving:

- Calories 153
- Fat 9 g
- Saturated fat 1 g
- Carbohydrates 18 g
- Fiber 5 g
- Protein 3 g
- Cholesterol 0 mg
- Sugars 7 g
- Sodium 146 mg
- Potassium 447 mg

Egg Salad

Here's a new way of making your favorite egg salad. In this recipe, we swap mayo with Greek yogurt. And instead of celery, we make it more flavorful with dill and green onions. We also add cucumber to the mix to make it more refreshing and to balance out the taste.

Serving size: 4

Preparation Cooking Time: 1 hour and 15 minutes

Ingredients:

- 4 hard-boiled eggs, chopped
- 1 cup cucumber, chopped
- ¼ cup plain Greek yogurt
- 1 teaspoon dried dill, crushed
- ½ cup green onions, chopped
- Salt and pepper to taste

Instructions:

1. Toss all the ingredients in a salad bowl.

2. Cover the bowl with foil.

3. Chill the salad for at least 1 hour before serving.

Nutrients per Serving:

- Calories 101
- Fat 6 g
- Saturated fat 2 g
- Carbohydrates 4 g
- Fiber 1 g
- Protein 9 g
- Cholesterol 188 mg
- Sugars 2 g
- Sodium 218 mg
- Potassium 146 mg

Egg Vegetable Salad

This egg and vegetable salad is perfect for a quick light lunch. In a few minutes, you can enjoy a healthy meal made with egg, carrots, scallions, cucumber and tomatoes.

Serving size: 4

Preparation Cooking Time: 25 minutes

Ingredients:

- 3 tablespoons light mayonnaise
- 3 tablespoons fat-free plain yogurt
- Salt and pepper to taste
- 8 hard-boiled eggs
- ½ cup cucumber, chopped
- ½ cup carrot, chopped
- ¼ cup scallions, sliced

Instructions:

1. Mix the mayo, yogurt, salt and pepper in a bowl. Set aside.

2. Slice the eggs and remove the yolks. Discard half of the yolks.

3. Combine the whites and remaining yolks in a bowl.

4. Mash and then stir in the rest of the ingredients.

5. Toss in the dressing and coat evenly.

Nutrients per Serving:

- Calories 135
- Fat 7 g
- Saturated fat 2 g
- Carbohydrates 7 g
- Fiber 1 g
- Protein 11 g
- Cholesterol 189 mg
- Sugars 3 g
- Sodium 248 mg
- Potassium 314 mg

Green Apple, Grapes Cabbage Salad

Chopped cabbage, halved grapes and slices of green apples coated with poppy seed dressing—this is one salad recipe you and your friends will surely find enticing.

Serving size: 12

Preparation Cooking Time: 1 hour and 15 minutes

Ingredients:

- 2 teaspoons honey
- ½ teaspoon poppy seeds
- ½ cup light mayonnaise
- 4 cups apple, sliced thinly
- 1 tablespoon lemon juice
- 1 ½ cups cabbage, chopped
- ¾ cup grapes, sliced in half
- ½ cup celery, sliced thinly

Instructions:

1. Make the dressing by mixing the honey, poppy seeds and mayonnaise.

2. In a large bowl, toss the apples in lemon juice.

3. Add the rest of the ingredients. Mix well.

4. Stir in the dressing. Coat evenly.

5. Chill for 1 hour before serving.

Nutrients per Serving:

- Calories 67
- Fat 3 g
- Saturated fat 1 g
- Carbohydrates 10 g
- Fiber 1 g
- Protein 0 g
- Cholesterol 4 mg
- Sugars 7 g
- Sodium 73 mg
- Potassium 92 mg

Shrimp Cobb Salad

If you're a fan of cobb salad, there's a good chance that you'd fall deeply in love with this recipe. It's a shrimp cobb salad that's made even more flavorful by Dijon dressing. When you look at the photo, it looks quite tedious to make but you'll be surprised that it will only you to 20 minutes to prepare this recipe.

Serving size: 4

Preparation Cooking Time: 20 minutes

Ingredients:

- 3 tablespoons white-wine vinegar
- 3 tablespoons olive oil
- 1 tablespoon Dijon mustard
- 2 tablespoons shallot, chopped
- Salt and pepper to taste
- 10 cups mixed salad greens
- 10 jumbo shrimp, cooked, peels and sliced in half lengthwise
- 1 cup cherry tomatoes, sliced in half
- 1 cup cucumber, diced
- 2 hard-boiled eggs, sliced
- 1 avocado, diced
- 2 slices bacon, cooked and chopped
- ¼ cup blue cheese, crumbled

Instructions:

1. Add the vinegar, olive oil, mustard, shallot, salt and pepper to a glass jar with lid.

2. Shake to blend well.

3. Arrange the salad greens on a plate.

4. Toss with half of the vinegar dressing.

5. Arrange the rest of the ingredients on top of the lettuce and pour the remaining dressing.

Nutrients per Serving:

- Calories 378
- Fat 25 g
- Saturated fat 6 g
- Carbohydrates 13 g
- Fiber 7 g
- Protein 29 g
- Cholesterol 243 mg
- Sugars 3 g
- Sodium 517 mg
- Potassium 1110 mg

Turkey Salad

Do you have leftover turkey from last night's dinner? Don't waste it. You can turn it into something beautiful and delicious like this turkey salad that's tossed with corn, strips of tortilla and bell pepper, made even more enticing with the drizzling of poppy seed dressing on top.

Serving size: 4

Preparation Cooking Time: 40 minutes

Ingredients:

- 1 tablespoon extra-virgin olive oil
- 1 tablespoon freshly squeezed lime juice
- ¼ cup freshly squeezed orange juice
- 1 teaspoon poppy seeds
- 1 tablespoon honey
- 2 corn tortillas, sliced into strips
- 1 teaspoon olive oil
- 2 cups corn kernels
- 6 cups Romaine lettuce, chopped
- 2 cups cooked turkey, sliced
- 2 tomatoes, chopped
- 1 red bell pepper, chopped
- 1 onion, sliced
- 3 strips turkey bacon, cooked and crumbled

Instructions:

1. Preheat your oven to 350 degrees F.

2. Mix the extra-virgin olive oil, lime juice, orange juice, poppy seeds and honey in a glass jar with lid.

3. Shake to blend well. Set aside.

4. Arrange the tortilla strips on a baking pan.

5. Bake in the oven for 10 minutes.

6. In a pan over medium heat, pour the oil and cook the corn for 8 minutes. Set aside.

7. Toss the rest of the ingredients in a salad bowl.

8. Pour the dressing over the salad.

9. Top with the corn and tortilla strips.

Nutrients per Serving:

- Calories 334
- Fat 8 g
- Saturated fat 2 g
- Carbohydrates 36 g
- Fiber 5 g
- Protein 32 g
- Cholesterol 76 mg
- Sugars 11 g
- Sodium 188 mg
- Potassium 846 mg

Cobb Salad in Mason Jar

Want to take your salad to work or when you go out? Make this layered cobb salad in a mason jar and chill in the refrigerator for a day until you're ready to eat it.

Serving size: 1

Preparation Cooking Time: 20 minutes

Ingredients:

- 2 tablespoons blue cheese dressing
- 2 tablespoons onion, diced
- 2 tablespoons cucumber, chopped
- 2 tablespoons tomato, chopped
- 1 oz. deli ham, chopped
- 1 oz. deli turkey, chopped
- 1 slice bacon, cooked and crumbled
- 1 hard-boiled egg, sliced into smaller pieces
- 1 teaspoon freshly squeezed lime juice
- ½ cup avocado, diced
- 2 cups Romaine lettuce, chopped
- 1 tablespoon blue cheese, crumbled

Instructions:

1. Pour the dressing into a mason jar.

2. Arrange in layers the following: onion, cucumber, tomato, ham, turkey, bacon and egg.

3. In a bowl, combine the lime juice and avocado.

4. Add as another layer to the jar.

5. Top with the lettuce and blue cheese.

6. Seal the jar.

7. Chill for one to two days.

8. Shake the jar before eating.

Nutrients per Serving:

- Calories 422
- Fat 28 g
- Saturated fat 7 g
- Carbohydrates 20 g
- Fiber 9 g
- Protein 25 g
- Cholesterol 227 mg
- Sugars 5 g
- Sodium 749 mg
- Potassium 929 mg

Fruit Salad

This is the perfect way to cap your meal—fruit salad coated with mayo and sour cream dressing. You can also serve this during snack time.

Serving size: 12

Preparation Cooking Time: 35 minutes

Ingredients:

- ¼ cup light mayonnaise
- ½ cup light sour cream
- 2 tablespoons freshly squeezed lime juice
- 1 tablespoon low fat milk
- 2 tablespoons sugar
- 1 teaspoon lime zest
- 1 cup mango, sliced into cubes
- 1 cup raspberries, sliced into cubes
- 1 cup pineapple chunks
- 1 cup strawberries, chopped
- 1 cup kiwi fruit, sliced

Instructions:

1. Make the dressing by mixing the mayo, sour cream, lime juice, milk, sugar and lime zest.

2. In a salad bowl, toss the fruits with the dressing.

Nutrients per Serving:

- Calories 64
- Fat 1 g
- Saturated fat 1 g
- Carbohydrates 13 g
- Fiber 2 g
- Protein 1 g
- Cholesterol 3 mg
- Sugars 5 g
- Sodium 61 mg
- Potassium 981 mg

Fruits in Honey Balsamic Dressing

Simple but satisfying—this delicious combination of grapefruits, kiwi and pears is one that you'd probably serve over and over at home. Making it even more special is the drizzling of honey balsamic dressing on top.

Serving size: 4

Preparation Cooking Time: 10 minutes

Ingredients:

- 1 pink grapefruit, sliced into sections
- 1 cup pear, sliced thinly
- 2 kiwi fruit, chopped
- 1 tablespoon honey
- 3 tablespoons balsamic vinegar

Instructions:

1. In a bowl, mix all the fruits.

2. Toss in the mixture of honey and vinegar.

Nutrients per Serving:

- Calories 83
- Fat 0 g
- Saturated fat 0 g
- Carbohydrates 21 g
- Fiber 3 g
- Protein 1 g
- Cholesterol 0 mg
- Sugars 14 g
- Sodium 2 mg
- Potassium 254 mg

Orange-Colored Fruit Salad

Here's a fun way of making fruit salad—use all the same colored ingredients! For this salad recipe, you combine all the orange-colored fruits that you can find.

Serving size: 8

Preparation Cooking Time: 15 minutes

Ingredients:

- 2 cups mango, diced
- 2 cups clementine, sliced into segments
- 2 cups cantaloupe, diced
- 1 cup yogurt
- 2 tablespoons freshly squeezed lime juice
- 1 tablespoon fresh mint, chopped

Instructions:

1. Add the mango, clementine and cantaloupe in a bowl.

2. Mix the yogurt and lime juice in another bowl.

3. Pour the yogurt dressing over the fruit salad.

4. Chill in the refrigerator for 30 minutes.

5. Sprinkle the chopped mint on top before serving.

Nutrients per Serving:

- Calories 53
- Fat 0 g
- Saturated fat 0 g
- Carbohydrates 13 g
- Fiber 2 g
- Protein 1 g
- Cholesterol 0 mg
- Sugars 11 g
- Sodium 7 mg
- Potassium 234 mg

Tomato Plum Kimchi Salad

This isn't like most salad dishes that you've tried before. This one is a combination of plums and tomatoes, seasoned with nori salt that you can make yourself.

Serving size: 6

Preparation Cooking Time: 15 minutes

Ingredients:

Dressing

- 2 tablespoons peanut oil
- 2 teaspoons low-sodium tamari
- 2 tablespoons rice vinegar
- 2 teaspoons sugar
- 1 ¼ teaspoons fish sauce
- 1 clove garlic, crushed and minced
- 3 tablespoons fresh ginger, sliced into strips
- ¼ teaspoon orange zest

Nori Salt

- ½ sheet nori seaweed
- 3 tablespoons sesame seeds
- ¼ teaspoon salt
- ½ teaspoon crushed red pepper

Salad

- 2 lb. tomatoes, sliced
- 2 plums, sliced into wedges
- 1 cup onion chives, chopped
- 1 cup cilantro, chopped

Instructions:

1. In a bowl, combine the oil, tamari, sugar and vinegar.

2. Stir in the rest of the dressing ingredients. Set aside.

3. In a pan over medium heat, toast the nori sheet for 2 minutes.

4. Tear into small pieces.

5. Put inside a spice grinder.

6. Pulse until powdery.

7. Transfer into a bowl.

8. Toast the sesame seeds in the same pan for 1 minute.

9. Add the salt, red pepper and sesame seeds to the nori powder. Mix well.

10. Toss the salad ingredients in a salad bowl.

11. Stir in the dressing and sprinkle with the nori salt.

Nutrients per Serving:

- Calories 104
- Fat 6 g
- Saturated fat 1 g
- Carbohydrates 12 g
- Fiber 3 g
- Protein 2 g
- Cholesterol 0 mg
- Sugars 7 g
- Sodium 268 mg
- Potassium 420 mg

Avocado Pineapple Salad

This is a Cuban inspired salad that is best served with saucy pork or chicken main dishes, or with beans and rice meals.

Serving size: 8

Preparation Cooking Time: 20 minutes

Ingredients:

- 2 avocados, sliced
- 1 pineapple, sliced into chunks
- 1 onion, sliced into rings and soaked in ice water for 10 minutes
- 3 tablespoons olive oil
- 1 tablespoon freshly squeezed lime juice
- Salt and pepper to taste

Instructions:

1. Combine the avocado, pineapple and onion in a salad bowl.

2. Mix the olive oil, lime juice, salt and pepper.

3. Toss the fruits in the dressing.

Nutrients per Serving:

- Calories 186
- Fat 13 g
- Saturated fat 2 g
- Carbohydrates 20 g
- Fiber 5 g
- Protein 2 g
- Cholesterol 0 mg
- Sugars 12 g
- Sodium 75 mg
- Potassium 374 mg

Grape Salad with Walnuts

Even though you love it, you avoid eating too much of grape salad as it is high in fat and sugar. You don't have to deprive yourself. You can make use of this recipe, which is healthier and much lower in both sugar and fat. But it tastes just as amazing.

Serving size: 12

Preparation Cooking Time: 20 minutes

Ingredients:

- Cooking spray
- ½ cup walnuts, chopped
- 2 teaspoons water
- Salt to taste
- 1 tablespoon brown sugar
- 3 tablespoons honey
- 4 oz. low-fat cream cheese
- 1 teaspoon vanilla
- ½ cup low-fat sour cream
- 6 cups grapes

Instructions:

1. Line your baking sheet with foil.

2. Spray it with oil.

3. Add the walnuts to a bowl.

4. Drizzle with the water.

5. Coat evenly with the salt and sugar.

6. Bake in the oven for 8 minutes or until brown. Let cool for 5 minutes.

7. Prepare the salad dressing by adding the honey, cream cheese, vanilla and sour cream into a food processor.

8. Pulse until smooth and creamy.

9. Toss the grapes in the honey mixture.

10. Sprinkle the candied walnuts on top and serve.

Nutrients per Serving:

- Calories 143
- Fat 7 g
- Saturated fat 2 g
- Carbohydrates 21 g
- Fiber 1 g
- Protein 2 g
- Cholesterol 11 mg
- Sugars 18 g
- Sodium 55 mg
- Potassium 198 mg

Conclusion

Salads are not only a feast for the eyes.

Their colors and textures are surely enticing but what make salads even more amazing are their numerous benefits for the health, as well as the fact that they are some of the simplest and easiest dishes to prepare.

Even if you lead a hectic lifestyle and you don't have much time to spare inside the kitchen, you surely won't have a hard time preparing a salad for yourself or for your family.

Cheers to a much healthier you!

About the Author

A native of Albuquerque, New Mexico, Sophia Freeman found her calling in the culinary arts when she enrolled at the Sante Fe School of Cooking. Freeman decided to take a year after graduation and travel around Europe, sampling the cuisine from small bistros and family owned restaurants from Italy to Portugal. Her bubbly personality and inquisitive nature made her popular with the locals in the villages and when she finished her trip and came home, she had made friends for life in the places she had visited. She also came home with a deeper understanding of European cuisine.

Freeman went to work at one of Albuquerque's 5-star restaurants as a sous-chef and soon worked her way up to head chef. The restaurant began to feature Freeman's original dishes as specials on the menu and soon after, she began to write e-books with her recipes. Sophia's dishes mix local flavours with European inspiration making them irresistible to the diners in her restaurant and the online community.

Freeman's experience in Europe didn't just teach her new ways of cooking, but also unique methods of presentation. Using rich sauces, crisp vegetables and meat cooked to perfection, she creates a stunning display as well as a delectable dish. She has won many local awards for her cuisine and she continues to delight her diners with her culinary masterpieces.

Author's Afterthoughts

I want to convey my big thanks to all of my readers who have taken the time to read my book. Readers like you make my work so rewarding and I cherish each and every one of you.

Grateful cannot describe how I feel when I know that someone has chosen my work over all of the choices available online. I hope you enjoyed the book as much as I enjoyed writing it.

Feedback from my readers is how I grow and learn as a chef and an author. Please take the time to let me know your thoughts by leaving a review on Amazon so I and your fellow readers can learn from your experience.

My deepest thanks,

Sophia Freeman

https://sophia.subscribemenow.com/

Printed in Great Britain
by Amazon